Fun Facts to Engage Students

Other Books by Jane C. Flinn

All Things History: Learning the Past with Fun Facts
(Rowman & Littlefield Publishers, March 2018)

All Things Science: Learning by Reading Fun Facts
(Rowman & Littlefield Publishers, July 2017)

Little Known Facts about the U. S. Presidents
(Rowman & Littlefield Publishers, November 2015)

Fun Facts to Engage Students

Questions to Inspire Thinking and Learning

Jane C. Flinn

ROWMAN & LITTLEFIELD
Lanham • Boulder • New York • London

Published by Rowman & Littlefield
An imprint of The Rowman & Littlefield Publishing Group, Inc.
4501 Forbes Boulevard, Suite 200, Lanham, Maryland 20706
www.rowman.com

Unit A, Whitacre Mews, 26-34 Stannary Street, London SE11 4AB

British Library Cataloguing in Publication Information Available

Library of Congress Cataloging-in-Publication Data

Names: Flinn, Jane, 1961- author.
Title: Fun facts to engage students : questions to inspire thinking and learning / Jane C. Flinn.
Description: Lanham, Maryland : Rowman & Littlefield, [2018]
Identifiers: LCCN 2018022699 (print) | LCCN 2018029457 (ebook) | ISBN 9781475845112 (Electronic) | ISBN 9781475845105 (pbk. : alk. paper)
Subjects: LCSH: Questions and answers.
Classification: LCC AG195 (ebook) | LCC AG195 .F56 2018 (print) | DDC 031.02—dc23
LC record available at https://lccn.loc.gov/2018022699

∞ ™ The paper used in this publication meets the minimum requirements of American National Standard for Information Sciences Permanence of Paper for Printed Library Materials, ANSI/NISO Z39.48-1992.

Printed in the United States of America

Contents

Preface

I have always had a thirst for knowledge, and that thirst has led me on a lifelong learning quest. The facts and figures I learned in school never seemed to be enough—I wanted to know it all.

One day, I walked into a local book store, picked up a trivia book, and couldn't put it down. I realized there was no better way to learn facts about countless subjects. I was learning not just those "main points" I learned in school—the ones you need to know for the test—but also the lesser-known/lesser-taught facts that gave topics depth and breadth.

The more I read, the more I learned—and that led me to combine my fascination with facts with my love for writing into a series of trivia books—including the one in your hands. With each book I've compiled, I've realized how much I still don't know.

I hope you learn something new every time you turn the page—I know I did.

Introduction

Trivia.

Unfortunately, the word has taken on a negative connotation, describing unimportant or inconsequential bits of information. I can't disagree more! What others may call trivial facts are, to me, a foundation for learning. They are the bricks and mortar that build knowledge. They can quench a thirst and spark curiosity.

Learning is not confined by time and space. With that in mind, this book is written for all ages, preschool to octogenarian, and can be used at any time, in any place. The multiple-choice, true/false, fill-in-the-blank, and open-ended questions offer information, encourage critical thinking, and provide an opportunity for readers of all ages to not only test their knowledge of a variety of topics but also learn something new along the way.

Parents and their children can read the book together, taking turns asking and answering questions. They can use the questions and answers as conversation starters at the dinner table, in the car, or while on a walk.

Classroom teachers can use the questions as daily warm-up activities or as a pre-assessment review. They might plan a game show activity around the questions—complete with contestants and prizes—or use the questions/answers as a basis for student research projects. The book's easy-to-read format and broad subject matter make it appropriate for all school levels, Pre-K–12, as well as higher education.

The book is a wonderful addition to the community library so community members of all ages can learn and enjoy the information. It's a fun and valuable resource at senior citizen centers, keeping seniors' minds active, jogging memories, and providing knowledge about what's going on in the world today.

The book's "Did You Know" facts offer a deeper dive into the topic to expand understanding and, I hope, spike curiosity.

Did Michelangelo sign his famous works of art?

What's a twillionnaire?

What bones were dug up when the Parthenon was being constructed?

You may know the answers to those questions—you may not. If you don't know the answers, do you want to?

Happy learning!

I

Categories

Science

1. What planet is the largest of all the terrestrial planets and is between Venus and Mars?
2. Matter is anything that has a mass, weight, volume, and takes up what?

    a. Space
    b. Time
    c. Energy

3. The main source of energy on Earth is the ________________.
4. A comet that crashes into Earth's atmosphere becomes a meteorite. True or false?
5. Huge hot balls of gas that are held together by gravity and give off their own light are called ________________.
6. Gold is the best conductor of electricity. True or false?
7. Solar power is used to generate electricity from what celestial object?

    a. Sun
    b. Moon
    c. Venus

8. Sunscreen protects the skin from what type of solar radiation?
9. Six hundred fifty million years ago, what kinds of fuel were formed from the decomposing remains of dead organisms?
10. What starts with an *a* and is made up of three particles: protons, neutrons, and electrons?

11. A chemical reaction is displayed on nails that are in which state?

    a. Being bent
    b. Rusting
    c. Being hammered into wood

12. Helium is the main greenhouse gas that is contributing to temperatures rising in the atmosphere. True or false?
13. On August 21, 2017, what celestial event was most of America looking at?
14. British sailors ate limes to prevent scurvy. This disease is caused by lack of what vitamin?
15. Food is measured in "these" that start with a "c."
16. The two common elements in seawater, sodium (Na) and chlorine (Cl), combine to make NaCl, which is what?

    a. Pepper
    b. Sugar
    c. Salt

17. DNA is present in white blood cells of humans, but not in _________________ blood cells, which lack nuclei.
18. A ballistic missile is a rocket that depends on gravity to reach its what?
19. Hypothesis is the name given to the longest side of a right-angled triangle. True or false?
20. Scientists believe that an asteroid impact and a surge in volcanic activity caused the wipeout of these reptiles sixty-five million years ago.
21. The outer crust of the earth is broken up into tectonic what?

    a. Plates
    b. Saucers
    c. Cups

22. Name this element that starts with an *n*, is used to make coins, and is also the main substance in Earth's inner core.
23. Absolute zero is the lowest possible temperature; nothing could be _________________, as no more heat can be removed from a substance.

Plants

1. Just like humans, plants get hungry. What process fuels them with energy that's necessary for their survival?
2. Saguaro is one of the most-recognized plants of the Sonoran Desert. What is it?

    a. Cactus
    b. Fern
    c. Tree

3. If you hear someone shouting "timber" in a forest, what is about to fall?
4. Plants are considered the "what" of the earth?

    a. Gall bladder
    b. Heart
    c. Lungs

5. Cypress ________________ root systems run underground, but some of their root structures come back up above ground.
6. Where would you find a frond?

    a. On a fern
    b. In the grass that surrounds a pond
    c. On the underbelly of a frog

7. Does seaweed have a root system?
8. A sassafras tree has three different shaped ________________.

9. What fruit looks like a pinecone?
10. The pitcher plant likes to trap and eat baseballs. True or false?
11. Some ponds are covered in duckweed. What color are these ponds?
12. Many modern medicines originally came from _______________.
13. What is the significance of the coast redwood tree?
14. What is the tallest grass in all the world?

    a. Elephant grass
    b. Bamboo
    c. Bermuda grass

15. What is one of the most-used plants in making clothing?
16. What is the "gas" in cranberries that causes them to bounce?
17. Where does the bulb of the onion grow?
18. What does the snapdragon flower resemble?
19. How many plant species have been identified?

    a. 2,000
    b. 20,000
    c. 200,000

20. Name this writing tool that is made from the incense-cedar tree.
21. Which tree is the one most often struck by lightning?
22. The best way to determine the age of a tree is to count its branches. True or false?
23. What's the only fruit that has seeds on its outside?
24. Name this grass in Africa that is high enough for an elephant to hide in.
25. The Durian fruit might be compared with skunk spray, as this is the world's _______________ fruit.

Animals

1. Squid and the eight-armed ________________ come from the family of cephalopods.
2. What does a koala bear have that a human being has as well—something that is considered a unique key to identity?

    a. Tongue print
    b. Fingerprint
    c. A big toe

3. The male lion does most of the hunting. True or false?
4. Name this mammal that sleeps with its incredibly long neck resting on its body.
5. The gradual development in which animals, humans, and other organisms have changed over time in order to survive is known as what?

    a. Symbiosis
    b. Cohabitation
    c. Evolution

6. Do wildebeests mate in the region of Kenya and Tanzania, or do they migrate there?
7. The Chow-Chow dog and the black bear share this tongue characteristic.
8. What insect accounts for 80 percent of pollination?
9. The Bedlington Terrier looks like a pony. True or false?
10. What type of animal is the arctic tern?
11. Name this mammal that has its own built-in suit of armor.

12. An octopus has eight arms and how many hearts?

    a. One
    b. Two
    c. Three

13. The "Ship of the Desert" is what animal?
14. In the song, what animals kept time with the Little Drummer Boy?
15. Name the political party that the elephant symbolizes.
16. The horseshoe fly is the fastest insect in the world. True or false?
17. The uakari excells as a tree climber in the Amazon rainforest. What type of animal is this?
18. Ladybugs aren't really bugs; they are ________________.
19. The koala bear feeds primarily on the red mulberry. True or false?
20. Which animal can be a gerenuk, gemsbok, or an oryx?

    a. Fish
    b. Bird
    c. Antelope

21. A bumble bee flutters its wings approximately 150 beats per ________________.
22. A snail breathes through what body part?

    a. Shell
    b. Foot
    c. Tentacles

23. The hippopotamus is the deadliest creature in the world. True or false?
24. New Zealand is home to 60 million what?

    a. Sheep
    b. People
    c. Exotic plants

25. Where are the lobster's teeth located?

Government

1. In the seventeenth century, how many "British Colonies" were on the east coast of North America?
2. Name the colony referenced above that starts with a *D*.
3. Eminent Domain is the right of _______________ to give money to a property owner to acquire real or personal property.
4. Who was the first female prime minister of the United Kingdom?

    a. Angela Merkel
    b. Portia Simpson Miller
    c. Margaret Thatcher

5. The Fifth Amendment of the U.S. Constitution guarantees Freedom of Religion and Freedom of Speech. True or false?
6. This U.S. government official can be elected for only two terms.
7. Name the highest ranking judicial body in the United States.
8. What are the first ten amendments to the U.S. Constitution called?
9. The Articles of Confederation preceded the U.S. Constitution. True or false?
10. What document declared the United States' independence from Great Britain?
11. _______________ is the legal power by the people in making the laws and regulations that affect the citizens of their country.
12. What type of government does North Korea have?

    a. Theocracy
    b. Communist dictatorship
    c. Oligarchy

13. On August 18, 1920, the Nineteenth Amendment to the U.S. Constitution granted African-American men the right to vote. True or false?
14. Anarchy, tyranny, and totalitarian are types of what?
15. A theocracy is a form of government in which ________________ is recognized as the supreme ruler.
16. Do stock markets tend to increase or decline over the course of a government shutdown?
17. What is the government system in which everyone is equal, receiving equal shares of the benefits derived from labor?
18. The collective term for the U.S. president's top advisors is what?

    a. Shelves
    b. Hangers
    c. Cabinet

19. The American ________________ has been a symbol of pride, hope, freedom, liberation, courage, inspiration, strength, and power.
20. The U.S. government is divided into six branches. True or false?
21. In 1776, it took Thomas Jefferson seventeen days to write what document?
22. There are two U.S. senators per state. How many senators does the nation have total?
23. Who owns almost half of all the land in the western United States?

    a. Native Americans
    b. U.S. federal government
    c. Casino tycoons

History

1. Native American Hopi tribes live on reservations, which is land that belongs to the government. True or false?
2. George Washington, Thomas Jefferson, and Samuel Adams all brewed their own what?

    a. Coffee
    b. Tea
    c. Beer

3. What was the first foreign company to start a factory in the United States?
4. What world-famous sharp shooter was born as Phoebe Anne Mozee?
5. St. Louis, Missouri, hosted the World's Fair to celebrate what event in 1803?
6. In 1903, what was sold for the first time for a nickel?

    a. Bottle of Coca-Cola
    b. Box of Crayola crayons
    c. Popsicle

7. After the Mexican War, the United States gained three states: New Mexico, California, and what other border state?
8. This was sent down a telephone line for the first time in 1876, and listening to it, you just might have wanted to put on your dancing shoes.
9. The first written mention of this legendary Scottish creature was made in 565 AD.

10. Although Nostradamus was famous for his many predictions, he was inaccurate with his forecasts of the two world wars. True or false?
11. How did Abraham Lincoln's mother, Nancy Hanks, die?

    a. Milk sickness
    b. Old age
    c. Measles

12. This famous inventor built the world's first coal-fired power station, Pearl Street Station.
13. In 1861, the University of Virginia was the United States' largest state school. In 1862, enrollment had dropped 90 percent because of this event.
14. In 1661, King Louis XIV was obsessed with building the Palace of Versailles, which sent this country into bankruptcy.
15. Why did the custom of shaking hands start?

    a. People wanted to show that they were free of any germs and that their hands were clean.
    b. It was a way to show respect.
    c. It proved they were unarmed.

16. The United Nations was established after World War II as a way to prevent what?
17. In 1931, criminal Al Capone started what kind of kitchen?
18. In the "running of the bulls," the papal bull is always the fastest. True or false?
19. What did Mary Ludwig Hays McCauley bring to soldiers during the American Revolutionary War?
20. The Dalai Lama is a vegetarian, like most Buddhist monks. True or false?
21. Amelia Earhart learned to do this before she could drive.
22. On July 4, 1776, the Founding Fathers signed the Declaration of Independence, and the "United States of America," was formed five years later. True or false?
23. In the olden days, people referred to their feet as dogs. This inspired the name for what shoe?

    a. Hush Puppies
    b. Chihuahuas
    c. Greyhounds

24. In ancient Greece, if a girl caught an apple that was being tossed to her, what did that signify?

    a. Her dream came true of becoming a teacher.
    b. She accepted a marriage proposal.
    c. She would have her own apple orchard.

25. Before the Parthenon was built, hundreds of wooly mammoth bones had to be cleared. True or false?

Geography

1. Asia is the largest continent. What is the second largest?
2. In what country is the monetary unit Thai Bhat used?
3. Denmark lies between Finland and Norway. True or false?
4. What is the capital of New Zealand?

    a. Wilmington
    b. Wellington
    c. Wilhomenia

5. There are six countries that surround the Black Sea. Name the one that is also a state in the United States.
6. The Andes Mountain Range is located in South America. True or false?
7. What percentage of Japan is covered in forests and mountains?

    a. 28 percent
    b. 75 percent
    c. 95 percent

8. What is the hottest continent?
9. What is the most linguistically diverse island country, with more than 852 different dialects?
10. The United States acquired Guam during the Spanish-American War. This was important, as it has a naval base in what ocean?
11. The only New England state without a seacoast is New Hampshire. True or false?
12. The capital of this country is Budapest.

13. Gibraltar is known as The Rock. What kind of English is spoken here?
14. Peru and this U.S. state have the sunflower in common as a symbol. What is this state?
15. South Korea uses which currency?

    a. Zloty
    b. Ruble
    c. Won

16. Norilsk, Russia, is the world's ______________ inhabited place, and Djibouti, Africa, is the world's hottest inhabited place.
17. How many time zones are in China?
18. In the United States, the longest street is Figueroa Street in Los Angeles, California. How long is it?
19. Has the Sahara Desert always been an arid desert?
20. In Canada, what is a loonie?

    a. Jumping marsupial
    b. Canadian dollar
    c. Frantic, crazy woman

21. Which country is east of Poland?

    a. Belarus
    b. Bulgaria
    c. Bogota

22. The term *heartland states* refers to those states that lie where in America?
23. West Virginia is known as what kind of a state?
24. It's easier to play baseball in Colorado's Rocky Mountains than elsewhere. True or false?
25. At 125,567 miles, Canada has the longest what in the world?

Technology

1. In the 1940s, computers were the size of a large room and used many watts of ________________.
2. In 1980, this cost $40,000, weighed 550 pounds, and the very first one was released into the world. What was it?
3. The first computer mouse was made of what material?

    a. Wood
    b. Mud that was hardened by drying in the sun
    c. Leather

4. What's the Internet information system invented by Sir Tim Burners-Lee in 1989?
5. Name this "horse" that is a virus yet pretends to be a useful program.
6. If you encounter a pop-up ad when you are online, what should you do?

    a. Share with your friends and show them how to get one
    b. Ignore it
    c. Call the doctor

7. A 1 with 100 zeros is known as what?
8. Java Script, HTML, and Python are all types of computer-programming languages. True or false?

9. The Nintendo company was founded in 1889 in Japan and originally sold what?

   a. Playing cards
   b. Toys, dolls, and building kits
   c. Wooden puzzles

10. Stealth technology makes an airplane _______________ to radar.
11. What is a machine that imitates a human and is guided by a computer program?
12. A mangonel was used by the military during medieval times to launch projectiles at what structure?
13. The first videocassette recorder (VCR) was the size of a toaster. True or false?
14. Plasma televisions create a picture from what kind of gas?
15. Nanotechnology deals with things that are extremely what?

    a. Small
    b. Big
    c. Unique

16. It took television thirteen years to reach a market audience of fifty million; radio reached this milestone many years before. True or false?
17. Ray Tomlinson sent the very first _______________ across the Internet in 1971, and there was no need for a stamp. What was it?
18. In the seventeenth century, what clock was commonly called the tall-case clock?
19. The first cell phone weighed two pounds and was called a Motorola DynaTAC 8000X. True or false?
20. Amazon sells more types of this book than printed books. What type of book is this?
21. A twillionaire is worth three times that of a billionaire. True or false?
22. What did Alfred Nobel use to blast through rock in 1866?
23. Which college dropout, along with Paul Allen, co-founded Microsoft?
24. What animal does the Google company rent to help cut down on the weeds and brush at their headquarters?

    a. Sheep
    b. Cows
    c. Goats

25. *Computer* was first used to describe a human who was able to perform what?

The Human Body

1. What do the red blood cells carry to all parts of the body?

    a. Nutrients
    b. Waste and other harmful bacteria
    c. Oxygen

2. Your calcaneus, talus, and navicular are all bones located in your skull. True or false?
3. There's a 1,000-foot-deep salt mine in the Ukraine that people visit. What are they being treated for?

    a. Respiratory ailments
    b. Infectious sores on the body
    c. Crohn's Disease

4. Cold compresses reduce the swelling of an ankle sprain. True or false?
5. What starts with an *a* and prevents cell damage caused by oxidants?
6. Your health is the most valuable thing you will ever possess. True or false?
7. On the human body, where is the axilla area?

    a. Back part of your knee
    b. Where your arm bends
    c. Underarm sweat gland

8. The "instructions" on how to make you are found in the nucleus of a cell. What are they called?

9. When one has a nose bleed, should one lean forward or back while pinching the nose?
10. The masseter muscle plays a major role in lifting the arm. True or false?
11. Every ten years, you have a new ________________, as bone cells are constantly being renewed.
12. Is every person's handwriting unique?
13. You can see your nose at all times, but what organ chooses to ignore it?

    a. Heart
    b. Liver
    c. Brain

14. A cup of coffee should be given to someone who might be having a heart attack. True or false?
15. Which organs remove excess water, salts, and other waste products from the blood?
16. Where is your jugular vein?
17. Name this main muscle of respiration.
18. What is the body's hardest-working muscle?

    a. Liver
    b. Brain
    c. Heart

19. Endorphins are the body's natural ________________ killers.
20. Expressing gratitude increases your happiness. True or false?
21. What organ in the human body uses the most energy?

    a. Liver
    b. Heart
    c. Brain

22. What's ten inches long and moves food from the throat to the stomach?
23. When bones come together, what do they form?
24. Is it safe to eat raw eggs?
25. All colors count when it comes to eating fruits and vegetables. True or false?

Entertainment

1. What type of instrument is the clarinet?
2. Is the main character in the book *Old Yeller* a grumpy old man?
3. What type of dog is Scooby-Doo?

    a. Old English Sheep Dog
    b. Great Dane
    c. Corgi

4. What Spanish artist could draw before he could talk?
5. In the popular book series *Curious George*, what type of animal is George?

    a. Vietnamese pot-bellied pig
    b. Alaskan mountain goat
    c. African monkey

6. What story is about a young boy growing up along the banks of the Mississippi River?
7. The Nimbus 2000 was Harry Potter's first ________________.
8. What was Rapunzel's main feature?

    a. Nails
    b. Hair
    c. Legs

9. The good wish said to an actor before his performance is "break an elbow." True or false?

10. "Have you ever heard the wolf cry to the blue corn moon or asked the grinning bobcat why he grinned?" These words are sung in what movie?
11. What type of instruments are the drums, xylophone, and cymbals?

    a. Percussion
    b. String
    c. Brass

12. In baseball, the ball should be gripped with two fingers and the ________________.
13. The color orange is created when red and white are mixed together. True or false?
14. In the movie *Frozen*, what is the name of the snowman?
15. Freckled-face Pippi Longstocking had superhuman what?
16. Eggs sink in water. To make them float, you add sugar. True or false?
17. Bees communicate by touch, smell, taste, and "this" that starts with a *d*.
18. Piglet, Roo, and Eeyore are friends with this lovable literary bear.
19. What do you call the group of men and women who sing together in four parts: soprano, alto, tenor, and bass?
20. In the fable "The Boy Who Cried Wolf," why didn't the townsmen believe the young shepherd even when he told the truth?
21. What birds are flying in the *Wizard of Oz* song "Somewhere Over the Rainbow"?

    a. Pink-tailed bunting
    b. Bluebirds
    c. Black-throated green warbler

22. What is Harry Potter's middle name?

    a. Winston
    b. Daniel
    c. James

23. Tom Hanks is the voice behind this cowboy in *Toy Story*.
24. Every day more money is printed for this "game" than for the U.S. Treasury. What is this game?

Potpourri

1. Name this calculation tool in which beads slide along a wooden frame.
2. What type of animal was captured in China and brought to the United States for the first time in 1936?
3. In 1839, Charles Goodyear vulcanized ________________ with sulfur.
4. What did Andre Michelin do to tires?
5. Which animal has the largest eyes in the animal kingdom?

    a. Octopus
    b. Rhinoceros
    c. Squid

6. What "bolts" can shoot out of an erupting volcano?
7. Levi Hutchins invented the ________________.
8. The Arctic is the continent with the fewest flowering plants. True or false?
9. Name this type of energy that starts with a *k*.
10. What is the major advantage of renewable energy?
11. Name this state that has more shoreline than the United States' entire Atlantic coast.
12. Bonsai is a method of grooming and training the growth of a ________________.
13. The cheapest seats at a bullfight are in the shade. True or false?

14. An epee, saber, and a falchion are what types of weapons?

    a. Swords
    b. Longbows
    c. Machine guns

15. In musical terminology, the term *piano* means to play in what way?
16. Cresta Run in Switzerland is a track for marathon runners. True or false?
17. What is the most slippery substance in the world?
18. What is the only change that takes place when water is put into the freezer?

    a. It changes color.
    b. It evaporates.
    c. It turns into ice.

19. What is the main purpose of the immune system?
20. An average cow in the United States produces how many gallons of milk per day?

    a. 8
    b. 19
    c. 28

21. What is the largest living thing on Earth?
22. Is a kinesthetic learner active or passive while learning?
23. What is the title of America's national anthem?
24. The "Pieta" is the only one of his works that Michelangelo signed. True or false?

II

Answers

Science

1. Earth

   Did You Know

   At 7,926 miles in diameter, our planet is a little bit larger than Venus. Mars comes in third at 4,222 miles in diameter.

   Earth's axis is angled, which allows the sun's energy into its atmosphere; if the sun's energy was not able to reach Earth because of its orbit, ice ages would occur.

2. a) Space
3. Sun

   Did You Know

   The primary source of the sun's energy is the nuclear fusion that occurs in the sun's core.

   The more massive a star is, the hotter it will be. Because it is so hot, it will burn more quickly and therefore die out more quickly.

   Blue stars are the hottest, and red stars are the coolest, although these are still very hot. Some stars, like our sun, are yellow. There's a scale on which stars are classified, and our sun is relatively cooler than other stars.

4. False. This is an asteroid. Once it hits earth, it becomes a meteorite, which consists mainly of rock.
5. Stars (including our sun).
6. False. The best conductor is silver (Ag).

Did You Know

Silver is the best metal conductor because the electrons are freer to move around than those of other elements.

7. a) Sun
8. Ultraviolet solar radiation.
9. Fossil fuel

Did You Know

It is not just the burning of coal that is damaging to our environment. The extraction, transportation, storage, and disposal all create environmental issues. For example, mining and burning coal significantly changes our environment, causing air pollution and climate change.

10. Atom

Did You Know

This is the basic building block of an element and cannot be broken down any further using any chemical means.

11. b) Rusting

Did You Know

When nails rust, a chemical reaction occurs as oxygen and iron combine to form a product called iron oxide or rust. A chemical reaction is when atoms split apart and are rearranged, forming new substances that have different properties.

12. False. It is carbon dioxide and methane.

Did You Know

Fossil fuels are coal, gas, and oil. These gases are called greenhouse gases because they trap heat in the atmosphere.

13. Total solar eclipse

Did You Know

Astronomers had predicted this great event happening in less than a second.

14. Vitamin C

Did You Know

In 1753, Scottish surgeon James Lind was the first to prove scurvy could be treated with citrus fruits.

Early shipping crews did not have a source of Vitamin C in their diets. They often sailed for many months and had no way of keeping foods fresh, as there was no refrigeration.

The Dutch sailors were given sauerkraut or zourkool, as they called it.

15. Calories

Did You Know
Calorie is a unit of measure for the energy in food.

16. c) Salt
17. Red

Did You Know
DNA is tightly wound and spread throughout the forty-six chromosomes. One set of twenty-three chromosomes is inherited from each parent. DNA exists inside these chromosomes, telling them what to be and what to do.

18. Target
19. False. This is the hypotenuse.
20. Dinosaurs

Did You Know
A huge explosion was made by this impact, which created a crater roughly 110 miles across. Debris from this explosion burst into the atmosphere, altering the climate severely. This led to the extinction of three-quarters of the species that existed at that time, including the dinosaurs.
This marked the end of the Cretaceous period and the entire Mesozoic era, opening the Cenozoic era as we know it today.

21. a) Plates

Did You Know
When these plates collide, it leads to strain or pressure; and when that's released, it causes earthquakes or volcanoes. This devastation is very important to our planet! Earth undergoes a process called "tectonic resurfacing," which allows fresh crust to form. This breaking-down process also allows carbon to be recycled. Without this action, our planet would not be able to sustain life.

22. Nickel
23. Colder

Did You Know
The coldest known object in the universe is the boomerang nebula, which has a temperature of –272 degrees Celsius; this is just one degree above absolute zero at –273 degrees Celsius.

Plants

1. Photosynthesis

   Did You Know

   Humanity and the ecosystems depend on this process. By using the energy from sunlight, plants convert water and carbon dioxide into sugar, oxygen, and starches.

2. a) Cactus

   Did You Know

   The Saguaro cactus is the largest cactus in the world.

   Gila woodpeckers drill holes to get to the water inside. To prevent water loss, the Saguaro seals off the hole with scar tissue.

3. Tree
4. c) Lungs

   Did You Know

   They are called this because they use the carbon dioxide from the atmosphere, and this purifies the atmosphere by releasing oxygen, which human beings breathe. In essence, our lungs keep us alive, and trees keep our lungs alive.

5. Trees

   Did You Know

   These roots that grow at right angles above the ground are called their "knees." These strange structures (also called pneumatophores) are found several feet away from the actual tree itself. They help the tree absorb oxygen from the air.

6. a) On a fern. This is the leafy part.

Did You Know

Ferns are among the oldest type of plant, on Earth for three hundred million years. Some species have remained unchanged for tens of millions of years.

7. No

Did You Know

Seaweed is algae, and algae does not need a root system in order to absorb water and nutrients. In the absence of a root system, they have "holdfasts," which anchor the seaweed to the sea floor.

Seventy percent of the world's oxygen comes from seaweed and other microscopic algae.

8. Leaves

Did You Know

One leaf is a normal shape, one is mitten shaped, and one has three segments—all on the same tree. The bark changes color from green into orange-brown as the tree gets older.

Root beer is made from this tree.

9. Pineapple

Did You Know

In 1398, pineapple was a name used for pinecones.

10. False. They like insects.

Did You Know

This carnivorous, meat-eating plant stores up a sweet-smelling juice that lures an insect to its mouth. Once the insect has sipped the juice, it is unable to climb back out and falls prey to this plant. This is how the pitcher plant gets its meal. This most mysterious leaf can also trap frogs, snakes, and birds!

11. Green

Did You Know

This easy-to-grow aquatic plant is a nutritious snack for water fowl, poultry, and fish.

12. Plants
13. World's tallest tree—also known as Sequoia

Did You Know

In 2006, Steve Sillett measured this tree in the most accurate way—by climbing to the top and dropping a tape measure straight to the ground.

14. b) Bamboo. It can grow thirty-five inches in a single day!

Did You Know

The panda is one of the world's most fascinating vegetarians. Their digestive systems have evolved to process meat, yet they eat nothing but bamboo—all day, every day!

15. Cotton

Did You Know

Bamboo and hemp are the other plants used in making clothes.

16. Air. It also causes them to float in water.

Did You Know

Dutch settlers nicknamed this fruit the "crane berry," as their blossoms resemble the neck of a sandhill crane.

17. Underground

Did You Know

All parts of the onion plant are edible, although the leaves can be toxic if eaten in large amounts.

18. Dragon

Did You Know

If the sides are squeezed, the "dragon's mouth" appears to open and close.

19. c) 200,000
20. Pencil

Did You Know

An average-size tree can provide enough wood to make one hundred seventy thousand pencils. About eighty-two thousand trees are cut each year to meet the demand of fourteen billion pencils.

21. Oak tree

Did You Know

Lightning's intense electrical current turns sap into steam in an instant. As a result, the tree may explode or split.

22. False. The best way is by counting the rings.

Did You Know

The science of calculating a tree's age is called dendrochronology.

23. Strawberry. It has approximately two hundred seeds.
24. Elephant grass

Did You Know

In Africa, this grass grows in dense clumps up to ten feet tall. Local farmers cut this grass for their animals, carrying it home on carts or in huge piles on their backs.

25. Smelliest

Did You Know

This fruit has such a potent stench that it's been banned from some hotels and mass transits in Asia. The smell has been described as turpentine, rotting meat, and gym socks.

Animals

1. Octopus
2. b) Fingerprints

Did You Know
Seventy million years' worth of evolution separates us from this adorable marsupial.

3. False. The female does 90 percent of the hunting.
4. Giraffe

Did You Know
A giraffe's neck can be over six feet in length.
It is the only animal that is born with horns; technically this is a bony protuberance.

5. c) Evolution
6. Migrate

Did You Know
Forced on by the power of the herd, the wildebeest have no choice but to take a suicidal plunge into crocodile-infested waters in which many thousands drown.

7. The color blue
8. Honeybee
9. False. It looks like a lamb.
10. Bird

Did You Know
The arctic tern makes the longest migration of any animal in the world.

11. Armadillo
12. c) Three

Did You Know
An octopus tires easily because its blood is copper-based.

13. Camel

Did You Know
Camels have three eyelids; this is to guard their eyes from blowing sand.
Despite the hump, a camel's spine is straight.

14. The ox and lamb
15. Republican
16. False. The dragonfly is the fastest.

Did You Know
Some dragonflies fly at speeds up to 98 mph. While in flight, they catch insects and mosquitoes.

17. Monkey

Did You Know
They are very striking with their bright-red face. The redder the monkey, the better chance it has of attracting a mate.

18. Beetles

Did You Know
The smell and taste of the ladybug is so horrible that once an insect tastes its yellow juice, it will never go after this insect again.

19. False. It eats Eucalyptus leaves.

Did You Know
The koala is not related to the bear in any way.

20. c) Antelope
21. Second
22. b) Foot

Did You Know
The snail moves around on a structure called a "foot"; this isn't really a foot, but rather a long muscular organ that is under its body.
Snails secrete mucus that helps them "glide" about.

23. False. The mosquito is far deadlier.

Did You Know

The mosquito carries a parasite called malaria; this disease kills one million people every year.

24. a) Sheep

Did You Know

The ratio of sheep to people is about seven sheep for every one person.

25. In its stomach

Did You Know

Lobster swallows its meal whole, and then the stomach does the chewing with its three "grinders" that look like molar teeth.

Government

1. Thirteen

    Did You Know
    In 1776, the thirteen colonies declared independence from Great Britain and formed the United States of America.

2. Delaware

    Did You Know
    The state bird of Delaware is the blue hen chicken; these are the fiercest of all the fighting roosters. During the Revolutionary War, soldiers would bring them out onto the battlefield for entertainment and inspiration.

3. Government
4. c) Margaret Thatcher

    Did You Know
    Margaret Thatcher served three consecutive terms in the twentieth century.
    This "Iron Lady" only got four hours of sleep at night.

5. False. It is the First Amendment.
6. President

    Did You Know
    The Twenty-Second Amendment to the Constitution set this limit on March 27, 1951. Before this date, there were no limits on how many times a president could be reelected.

7. Supreme Court

Did You Know
Justices are appointed for life but can be impeached.

8. The Bill of Rights
9. True. In 1789, the U.S. Constitution as we know it today went into effect.

Did You Know
Under the Articles of Confederation, John Hanson was the first president of the "United States in Congress Assembled." George Washington was the first president under the U.S. Constitution that we follow today.

10. The Declaration of Independence
11. Government
12. b) Communist dictatorship
13. False. This amendment ended the women's suffrage movement in the United States and allowed women to vote.

Did You Know
Although women were granted the right to vote in 1920, they did not turn out to the polls in the same numbers as men until 1980. From this time until the present, women have voted in elections in the same percentage as men and sometimes more.

14. Government
15. God
16. Decline

Did You Know
Since 1976, the government has shut down eighteen times.

17. Communism

Did You Know
In Communism, everything is shared equally.
The founding father of modern Communism is Karl Marx.

18. c) Cabinet

Did You Know
Cabinet members are some of the most powerful people in the United States. They are chosen by the president and confirmed by the Senate.

19. Flag

Did You Know

America is a symbol of freedom, as we have liberties and rights that other countries do not have.

20. False. Our federal government is divided into three branches.

Did You Know

These branches are the legislative, executive, and judicial. The legislative branch is made up of the House and Senate, and the collective term is *Congress*.

21. Declaration of Independence
22. One hundred
23. b) U.S. federal government

Did You Know

As the United States expanded across the continent, it was taking the land (that would become new states) from the Native Americans.

History

1. False. The hopis live on land which they own and control; they also have their own government. However, they are U.S. citizens and, therefore, must obey American law.

   Did You Know
   Hopi is pronounced "hope-ee," and translates into peaceful person.

2. c) Beer
3. Volkswagen
4. Annie Oakley

   Did You Know
   Her amazing talent was noticed at age fifteen. She joined Buffalo Bill's Wild West Show a few years later.

5. Louisiana Purchase

   Did You Know
   Louisiana was the launching point for Louis and Clark's expedition. Their trail travels took them to St. Louis, Missouri.

6. b) Box of Crayola crayons

   Did You Know
   The first box of Crayola crayons consisted of eight colors.

7. Texas
8. Music

   Did You Know
   This was the same year that the telephone was invented.

9. Loch Ness Monster

Did You Know
She was first spotted by St. Columba as he took a swim in Loch Ness—the largest body of fresh water in Britain.

10. False

Did You Know
When he was in his forties, Sir Michel de Nostredame would go into a meditative state and have visions of the future. He documented these visions, and in 1558 published his famous *The Prophecies*.

11. a) Milk sickness

Did You Know
Because there was no grass on the Lincolns' farm, the cows ate snakeroot, which poisoned the milk, which Nancy drank. Abe's aunt and uncle died from this same illness.
Others suggest that Nancy died of consumption or tuberculosis.

12. Thomas Edison

Did You Know
Edison liked to go camping with his friend Henry Ford, the auto tycoon.

13. Civil War
14. France

Did You Know
King Louis XIV did not care about the cost of the palace or the welfare of his workers. More than thirty thousand worked on this building, and many lives were lost during construction.

15. c) It proved they were unarmed.
16. War
17. Soup

Did You Know
Al Capone started this to clean up his image and to feed Chicago's needy.

18. False. A papal bull is a type of letter issued by the pope of the Catholic church.
19. Water

Did You Know
This earned her the nickname "Molly Pitcher." She was very brave, as she was often under heavy military fire from the British troops.

20. False. He eats meat.

Did You Know

The Dalai Lama was born Lhamo Dhondup, then renamed Tenzin Gyatso. At the tender age of six, he became a monk. "His Holiness" wakes up at 3:30 a.m. and meditates for the first five hours of the day, taking a break for breakfast. If he hadn't been a monk, he would have been an engineer.

21. Fly

Did You Know

Her biplane was yellow, so she named it Canary.

"Please know that I am aware of the hazards. I want to do it because I want to do it." —Amelia Earhart

22. True

Did You Know

Our nation became the United States of America in March 1781.

23. a) Hush Puppies
24. b) She accepted a marriage proposal.
25. False. These were dinosaur bones.

Geography

1. Africa
2. Thailand

    Did You Know
    The world's smallest mammal, the bumblebee bat, is found in Thailand.

3. False. Sweden is between Finland and Norway.
4. b) Wellington

    Did You Know
    New Zealand has an official sign language, NZSL.

5. Georgia
6. True
7. b) 75 percent
8. Africa

    Did You Know
    Most of this continent is made up of deserts.

9. Papua New Guinea
10. Pacific

    Did You Know
    The beaches of Guam are covered in ground coral rather than sand.

11. False. It is Vermont.
12. Hungary

Did You Know

Hungarian engineer Erno Rubik invented the famous logic-toy, Rubik's Cube. This was originally called Magic Cube.

13. Rock English
14. Kansas
15. c) Won
16. Coldest
17. One

Did You Know

Although, this country could have five different time zones, the government requires that all clocks in this nation conform to those in the capital of Beijing.

18. Thirty miles
19. No

Did You Know

Before the Ice Age, there were grasslands, lakes, and streams, and animals were plentiful.

20. b) Canadian dollar
21. a) Belarus

Did You Know

Belarus borders Latvia, Lithuania, Poland, and Russia.

22. Midwest
23. Panhandle

Did You Know

There are nine "panhandle" states.

24. True

Did You Know

The higher you are above sea level, the thinner the air gets. If you throw a ball up in these mountains, it will go farther than at lower elevations.

25. Coastline

Did You Know

Indonesia's coastline is second at 33,998 miles.

Technology

1. Electricity
2. First modern computer

Did You Know
You blink twenty times a minute, but only seven times a minute when you are using a computer.

3. a) Wood
4. World wide web
5. Trojan horse
6. b) Ignore it
7. Googol

Did You Know
This is where the company Google gets its name.
Larry Page and Sergey Brin started Google in a friend's garage in Menlo Park, California.

8. True
9. a) Playing cards. The cards were called Hanafuda cards.

Did You Know
Nintendo was founded by Fusajiro Yamauchi and was originally called Nintendo Koppai.

10. Invisible
11. Robot

Did You Know
George Charles Devol invented the first industrial robot, called Unimate.

12. Castle wall
13. False

Did You Know

In 1956, the VCR was the size of a piano.

14. Plasma
15. a) Small

Did You Know

This is a science that deals in atoms and molecules.

16. False

Did You Know

It took radio thirty-eight years to reach a market audience of fifty million.

17. Email

Did You Know

Computer engineer Ray Tomlinson sent this across ARPANET, an early version of the Internet. "It was not an assignment; he was just fooling around," said a colleague about Ray's invention of email.

18. Grandfather clock

Did You Know

In 1875, when a song titled "My Grandfather's Clock" became popular, the tall-case clock came to be called the grandfather clock.

19. True

Did You Know

This phone, invented in 1984, sold for $4,000. It was so big and heavy that its creators nicknamed it "the brick."

Charging it took ten hours for thirty minutes of use.

20. e-book
21. False. A twillionaire is a Twitterer with a million followers.
22. Dynamite that he invented

Did You Know

Alfred mixed nitroglycerin with silica, and this liquid formed into a paste called dynamite. This Swedish industrialist built bridges and buildings in his native country.

The Nobel Prize is named for him.

23. Bill Gates

Did You Know

Bill's home was designed using a Macintosh computer.

The first Apple logo featured scientist Sir Isaac Newton sitting under a tree with an apple about to fall on his head.

24. c) Goats

Did You Know

More than two hundred goats chomp away on grassy goodness at their Mountain View headquarters.

25. Calculations

The Human Body

1. c) Oxygen
2. False. They are bones of the lower leg.
3. a) Respiratory ailments

Did You Know

The trachea, or windpipe, branches into the bronchi, which are two tubes that carry air into each lung.

4. True
5. Antioxidants

Did You Know

These are found in fruits, vegetables, and chocolate (to name a few).

6. True

Did You Know

People who regularly eat meals in restaurants double their risk of becoming obese.

7. c) Underarm sweat glands
8. DNA

Did You Know

You have ten trillion cells in your body. If the DNA in all the cells were stretched out, they would stretch 744 million miles—to the moon and back one thousand five hundred times!

9. Forward
10. False

Did You Know

This connects the lower jawbone to the cheekbone and plays a major role in chewing food.

11. Skeleton
12. Yes

Did You Know

Your handwriting is controlled by your unconscious mind.

13. c) Brain

Did You Know

Your brain is 80 percent water and is most active when you are sleeping!

14. False. An aspirin should be given.

Did You Know

An aspirin can reduce blood clotting in potential heart-attack victims.

15. Kidneys

Did You Know

Your renal arteries supply your kidneys with blood.

16. In your neck

Did You Know

These two main veins return blood from the head, brain, face, and neck to the heart.

17. Diaphragm

Did You Know

This large muscle is located just beneath the lungs and plays a vital role in the breathing process.

When it suddenly spasms into a series of uncontrollable intakes of air, you get hiccups.

18. c) Heart

Did You Know

It pumps out two ounces of blood at every heartbeat.

19. Pain

Did You Know

Endorphins are the feel-good brain chemicals.

Endorphins, adrenaline, serotonin, and dopamine are released when you exercise. Exercising when you are young will improve your brain function when you are older.

20. True
21. c) Brain

Did You Know

The average brain weighs three pounds and uses 20 percent of the body's energy.

22. Esophagus

Did You Know

This eight-inch-long tube is made of muscles that contract to push the food through to the stomach. This process is called peristalsis.

23. A joint
24. No

Did You Know

Eggs may contain the bacteria salmonella. Cookie dough should not be eaten, as it is made with raw eggs.

25. True

Entertainment

1. Woodwind

    Did You Know
    The clarinet descended from the French instrument, the chalumeau.

2. No. It's about a yellow dog.
3. b) Great Dane

    Did You Know
    Scooby Doo is supposed to be a Great Dane, although typically Great Danes don't have his coloration.

4. Pablo Picasso

    Did You Know
    This child prodigy's first word was *lapiz*. This is the Spanish word for pencil.
    He owned a variety of animals, including a pet monkey.

5. c) African monkey

    Did You Know
    Curious George was published in 1941. At this time, King George was the king of England. In England, out of respect for the king, Curious George was called Zozo.

6. *The Adventures of Tom Sawyer*

    Did You Know
    Mark Twain was the pen name of author Samuel Langhorne Clemens.

7. Broom

8. b) Hair

Did You Know

Rapunzel had hair that was the length of her tower. She also had a pet chameleon.

9. False. It's "break a leg."
10. *Pocahontas*
11. a) Percussion
12. Thumb

Did You Know

It is important to be set and balanced when making a throw.

13. False. It's pink.
14. Olaf
15. Strength

Did You Know

In the movie, Pippi is nine years old, and she does not put up with being bullied.

16. False. Add lots of salt.

Did You Know

Eggs float in salt water because it is denser than fresh water.

17. Dance

Did You Know

Bees must visit two million flowers to yield one pound of honey.

18. Winnie the Pooh
19. Choir
20. He had lied to them before.
21. b) Bluebirds

Did You Know

Although, this film was popular in 1939, it was overshadowed by the movie *Gone with the Wind. Wizard of Oz* cost so much to produce that it didn't turn a profit until it was re-released in 1948.

22. c) James
23. Woody
24. Monopoly

Did You Know

Parker Brothers prints $50 billion of Monopoly money yearly.

The United States Bureau of Engraving prints thirty-eight million notes with a value of $541 million a day.

Potpourri

1. Abacus
2. Giant panda cub

Did You Know

Su Lin was plucked from the jungles of Asia and for two months swept around the planet on airplanes and sea ships, landing in New York City. American reporters at Grand Central Station reported every bit of news about her trip across the Pacific.

3. Rubber

Did You Know

Before Charles patented rubber in 1844, he was a merchant who went bankrupt and was imprisoned due to debt.

4. Put air in them
5. c) Squid

Did You Know

A squid's eyes can be as large as sixteen inches across.

6. Lightning

Did You Know

Lightning occurs mostly during the part of the eruption when the large volcanic plumes are shooting out.

7. Alarm clock. He didn't want to oversleep.

Did You Know

The alarm clock rang only at 4:00 a.m., as this was the time Levi wanted to wake up at. This was the first mechanical alarm clock invented in America in 1787.

8. False. It is Antarctica.
9. Kinetic
10. It will never run out.
11. Michigan

Did You Know

The state's official stone is petoskey. This is found along the shores of Lake Michigan.

12. Tree

Did You Know

The Chinese and Japanese have their own art of growing this tree.

13. False. Ringside seats in the shade are the most expensive seats.

Did You Know

This is because most of the action takes place in the shade and it is the most comfortable place to be in the summer's heat.

14. a) Swords
15. Softly
16. False. It is an ice-skeleton toboggan track.

Did You Know

Every year since 1885, this ice chute has been made with snow that is then iced.

17. Teflon

Did You Know

This is the same substance on nonstick cookware.

18. c) It turns into ice.

Did You Know

There are at least seventeen different types of ice. Ice forms under different conditions and temperatures and takes on different shapes and sizes. Ice in the freezer is known as Ice IV. Some ice will actually sink if put into a glass of water!

19. Fight against diseases
20. a) 8
21. Australia's Great Barrier Reef

Did You Know

This reef stretches 1,429 miles, and it is visible from space.

22. Active
23. The Star-Spangled Banner
24. True

Did You Know

After placing this magnificent sculpture in Saint Peter's Basilica, Michelangelo overheard a man comment that it was done by another artist. That night, Michelangelo used a hammer and chisel to inscribe his full name. He regretted doing this and vowed never again to sign a work of his.

About the Author

Jane C. Flinn, the "Queen of Trivia," is a creative writer from Vero Beach, Florida, and the author of several trivia books, including *The Best Trivia Book Ever*.